theology
MY

Duppy
Conqueror

theology
MY

Robert Beckford

Duppy Conqueror

Fortress Press

Minneapolis

DUPPY CONQUEROR

Originally published by Darton, Longman, and Todd
London, UK

Print ISBN: 978-1-5064-8439-6
eBook ISBN: 978-1-5064-8440-2

Cover design: Kristin Miller

Contents

Introduction

MY THEOLOGY TAKES inspiration from the emancipation/defiance tradition of African Caribbean Christianity.

Black Christians of African Caribbean heritage in Britain are inheritors of two distinct Christian traditions. The first is the colonial Christian theology of the Anglican, Methodist and Baptist missionaries to the slave and colonial societies of the so-called 'West Indies'. Colonial Christianity was theologically dishonest – it taught a distorted version of the Christian gospel to make consistent the gospel of Jesus Christ with racial capitalism (slavery) and slavery's racial terror (race and sexual violence). Arguably, the publication of the *Slave Bible* in 1807 in London by an obscure Church of England missionary society is the high point of colonial Christianity's complicity with false doctrine – redacting the whole of Holy Scripture into a legitimation for white supremacist mythology takes some beating![1] The second inheritance is the Christianity of the enslaved and later colonial subjects. Many, but not all, enslaved Africans rejected missionary Christianity's lies about God.[2] Enslaved Africans re-made the gospel by combining liberative fragments of memory of freedom from the African past to their interpretation of the Bible to create an emancipatory God-talk. Emancipatory God-talk describes ideas about God that resist the consigning of black flesh to the second-class category of 'Christian slavery'.[3] For enslaved Africans, God was an emancipator and the enslaved, like the Hebrews in Egypt, expected divine intervention, supernatural or natural, for their freedom from colonial bondage.

These two Christian traditions, one white

[1] Mills, David Charles, *Unholy: The Slaves Bible* (London: Ghetto Kids Enterprises, 2009).
[2] Stewart, N. D., *Three Eyes for the Journey* (Oxford University Press, 2005).
[3] Wilmore, Gayraud S., *Black Religion and Black Radicalism An Interpretation of the Religious History of African Americans* (Maryknoll, N.Y.: Orbis Books, 2012).

supremacist and the other black emancipatory, reside concurrently in African Caribbean Christianity in Britain: a double consciousness of deference and defiance. These two traditions are not mutually exclusive; they intersect in complex ways[4] but rarely in a modality of expression which foregrounds emancipation/ defiance. The latter, emancipation/defiance, is the object of my theological orientation. I say 'orientation' because my desire was never to craft a systematic theology, but instead provide a scaffold for a dynamic equivalent of the emancipation/defiance tradition of Caribbean Christianity. In short, I gesture towards a black British constructive theology of black emancipation.

Malcolm, Rastafari, and Cone

Three formative experiences inform my theological orientation. These are: reading *The Autobiography of Malcolm X*; reasoning with

---

[4] Alexander, Valentina, *Breaking Every Fetter? To What Extent Has the Black Led Church in Britain Developed a Theology of Liberation?* (University of Warwick, 1998).

Rastas; and encountering the black liberation theology of James Cone.

The first experience was as a fifteen-year-old schoolboy, reading *The Autobiography of Malcolm X.* It was a white, middle-class schoolteacher who introduced me to Malcolm X during a maths class in my inner-city comprehensive school. The maths teacher referred to Malcolm X to illustrate the meaning of 'X' in maths as a register for the unknown. I was fascinated by this brief, tangential introduction to black radicalism and decided to borrow a copy of *The Autobiography of Malcolm X* from the local library. The year was 1980, and a decade before the renaissance in interest in Malcolm X's life and thought, concurrent with Spike Lee's epic filmic representation in 1992.[5] *The Autobiography* had an immediate impact on my emerging spirituality. Malcolm's triangulation of criticism of white racism in America, the collusion of Christianity with racial terror,

---

[5] Spike Lee, *Malcolm X* (Forty Acres, and a Mule, 1992)·

and the necessity of a psychic conversion to 'blackness' inadvertently alerted me to the coloniality of my Christianity – the deference tradition in my own faith experience.

The second experience was conscientization by Rastafarians. The summer term of the same year, 1980, like clockwork, I caught the same bus home daily to cross paths with a group of 'dreads' returning from a day's work. The precision timing was necessary to take part in a 'reasoning session' or what Rastafarians describe as 'grounding' on the top of the No. 21 bus from Coventry city centre. The conversation, mostly convivial and occasionally tense, was for me a part history lesson, an introduction to black cultural studies and initiation into the Caribbean's first black liberation theology rolled into one. The Rastas 'schooled' me in an alternative black religious history, a pantheon full of men and women who appropriated religion to pursue black freedom. The Rastas also spoke of the black Christian revolutionaries Sam Sharpe, and Paul Bogle and the conflictual, contradictory history of the Jamaican Maroons, including the famous Maroon warrior-priestess, Nanny. Regarding black cultural studies, Rastafarian 'dread talk' communicated the availability of a rich reservoir of religious ideas and concepts within Jamaican culture. I was intrigued by the concepts of 'dread', 'Ital', 'dub', and 'rahtid'. Later in my career, I would incorporate aspects of the Jamaican language into my theological reasoning and vocabulary. Finally, the Rastas articulated a holistic soteriology. A vision of God's work in the world that included historical wrongdoing (reparations for slavery), the emancipation of oppressed people ('free South Africa' was one of the Rastas' regular refrains) and a black deity (Haile Selassie I). The Rastas' schooling was de-facto a short-course in the emancipation/defiance tradition.

These first two formative experiences created a thirst for a Christian theology that does the work of racial justice and black empowerment. My hunger was satisfied when I encountered the books of the patriarch of black liberation theology, James Cone (1938-2018).

INTRODUCTION

I read James Cone's *Black Theology and Black Power* (1969) as an undergraduate student in New York State in the mid-1980s. As an overseas scholarship student, I soaked up everything the African-American intellectual tradition had to offer – including the emerging black liberation theology. Cone's analysis of western Christian theology laid bare the history of Christian collusion with racial terror and the necessity of black theology to manufacture a theology contemporaneous with the black struggle for freedom in America and abroad. As I note in my radio documentary *Black Jesus* (BBC World Service 2020),[6] for black and womanist (black Christian feminist) theologians of my generation, James Cone's books were a source of inspiration, and within the particularity of my experience gave rise to the idea of a contextual black liberation theology, or what Caribbean theologians term 'emancipatory theology'.[7]

[6] See *Black Jesus* (BBC World Service, 2020), https://www.bbc.co.uk/programmes/w3ct1cw9
[7] Davis, Kortright, *Emancipation Still Comin': Explorations in Caribbean Emancipatory Theology* (Eugene, Oregon, Wipf & Stock, 2008).

My postgraduate studies at the University of Birmingham in England in the 1990s provided an opportunity to develop this new theological trajectory. A scholarly precedent existed, and I was able to build on the work of British pioneers in this field.[8] Also, I received incredible support from the African American theologians, Randall Bailey, Jacquelyn Grant, Renita Weems and Anthony Pinn. All responded to the 'Macedonian call' of the pioneering developments of Black Theology in Britain and travelled to the UK to lecture at events at the Queen's College and the University of Birmingham in the 1990s. James Cone delivered a game-changing lecture in the mid-1990s at the Queen's College that almost singlehandedly bulldozed an intellectual pathway through the barricade of stodgy, abstract, esoteric British theological methodological norms. My PhD thesis, however, moved in a discrete direction; it correlated aspects of

---

[8]   Grant, Paul, and Patel, Raj, *A Time to Speak: Perspectives of Black Christians in Britain* (Birmingham: CRRU, 1990); Grant, Paul, and Patel, Raj, *A Time to Act: Kairos 1992* (Birmingham [England]: [Evangelical Christians for] Racial Justice).

African Caribbean Pentecostal thought with Rastafari belief and practice to envision ideas about God to emancipate black British people from the enslavement of the oppressive tradition of  colonial Christianity. The publication, *Dread and Pentecostal: A Political Theology for the Black Church in Britain* (2000), was the fruit of my postgraduate labour. Personally speaking, the ideas in the book were more than an abstraction. The publisher SPCK's original front cover depicts a self-portrait that captures my flowing dreadlock hairstyle, which signified the embodiment of emancipatory theology. As Stuart Hall notes, the black body has always been a canvas for black thought.[9]

---

[9] Hall, Stuart, 'What Is This "black" in Black Popular Culture?', *Stuart Hall: Critical Dialogues in Cultural Studies*, 455 (1997).

Theology and Cultural Studies

Since my post-graduate research days, I have continued to develop emancipatory theology across a range of media. Four discrete methodologies inform my theological orientation. These are correlation cultural studies, intertextuality, and praxis.

The first method is Paul Tillich's correlation.[10] Correlation in its simplest form describes a question and answer relationship between theology and the social world. Correlation, as an embrace of a broader theological worldview, has resonance with the inclusive impulse in African and African Caribbean spirituality.[11] As a feature of Caribbean culture, Caribbean spirituality

[10] Clayton, John Powell, *The Concept of Correlation: Paul Tillich and the Possibility of a Mediating Theology* (Berlin: Walter de Gruyter, 1980); Wariboko, Nimi, and Yong, Amos, *Paul Tillich and Pentecostal Theology: Spiritual Presence and Spiritual Power* (Bloomington: Indiana University Press, 2015).

[11] Mbiti, John S., *Concepts of God in Africa* (Nairobi, Kenya: Acton Publishers, 2012); Sutherland, Patsy, Moodley, Roy and Chevannes, Barry, *Caribbean Healing Traditions: Implications for Health and Mental Health* (New York: Routledge, 2014).

refuses occidental theology's separation of the sacred and secular.[12] Rastafari, born from the soil of Caribbean spirituality, has a similar conversational method; a dialogic theological imagination traversing between social concerns and the Bible to make sense of the black predicament ('citing up'). In terms of my interest in emancipatory theology, correlation provided a framework for engaging in creative conversations between categories such as 'God,' 'Jesus,' and the 'Holy Spirit' in aspects of African Caribbean diaspora experience and culture in Britain.

Unlike western philosophy, the traditional dialogue partner for British theology, cultural studies contends with structural issues such as race, class, and gender. Consequently, cultural studies textbooks published in the 1980s and 1990s in Britain regularly contemplated racial politics. Black cultural politics, diasporic identity, the criminal justice system, and the dynamics of black feminism were a few of the

[12] Riggs, Marcia, and Logan, James Samuel, *Ethics that Matters: African, Caribbean, and African American Sources* (Minneapolis: Fortress Press, 2012).

salient topics.[13] Yet few if any of these categories were inside of the machinates of western philosophy, and the omission has catastrophic outcomes for British theology. At the time of writing only two books have been written about theology and 'race' by white British theologians, and there are twice as many African Caribbean people teaching in one department of sociology in Birmingham (the Department of Sociology and Criminology at Birmingham City) than the nationally combined figures of all the African Caribbean academics teaching theology in British universities.[14] Arguably, with such

[13] Gilroy, Paul, *The Black Atlantic: Modernity and Double Consciousness* (Cambridge, Mass: Harvard University Press, 1993); *The Empire Strikes Back: Race and Racism in 70s Britain* (London: Hutchinson, 1982).

[14] Wilkinson, John L., *Church in Black and White: The Black Christian Tradition in 'Mainstream' Churches in England: A White Response and Testimony* (Edinburgh: Saint Andrew Press, 1993); Leech, Kenneth, *Churches fighting racism in the '80s* (Cambridge: Great St Mary's, the University Church, 1987). In 2021 there were only two African Caribbean heritage academics teaching theology in the UK at British Universities. At the same time, the Department of Sociology and Criminology at Birmingham City University had more than four African Caribbean heritage members of staff.

little reflection on 'race', Christian theology in Britain is the most 'colonized' discipline within the major Humanities subjects. Returning to my approach. When placed in dialogue with cultural studies, emancipatory theology made possible theological reflection on various social issues confronting the black community, including violent racial attacks, mental health and the quest for social justice.

Another method is Intertextuality. Intertextuality is an integral feature of my theology because of my work as a media professional. In addition to my academic career, since the late-1990s, I have also worked in radio and television broadcasting. Living the intersection of teaching and making radio and television programmes allows me to entangle emancipatory theological ideas with broadcasting content. Another way of conceiving this process is to view my media texts as a theological 'war of positioning' – the waging of a black theological struggle to win hearts and minds across various social concerns in Africa, the Caribbean and Britain.

In 2017, I extended the reach of this approach to incorporate contemporary gospel music.[15]

Finally, praxis seeks to connect thought and action so that ideas never remain ethereal, but are made concrete and material. Regarding theology, praxis refers to the incorporation of action in all theologizing. Praxis in theology is committed to transformation, whether described as the 'action-reflection model', 'the hermeneutical spiral', or theological reflection. Praxis is not a new idea in African Caribbean Christianity. The contextual experience of the inclusive impulse and colonial oppression orient at least one tradition within African Caribbean Christianity (defiance) towards action in the social world.

In my theology, praxis is twofold – played out in scholar activism and the direct political action made possible by the intertextuality of theology and media. Regarding scholar activism, I have always thought that my

[15] See https://www.canterbury.ac.uk/arts-and-humanities/ school-of-humanities/religion-philosophy-and-ethics/ research/jamaican-bible-remix.aspx

personal success should be measured by the number of black students and colleagues I support and develop in black theology, than the number of publications I produce or accolades and awards I receive. In the words of my Jamaican parents, as an educator I underline the Afri-centric commitment to mass education, colloquially expressed in the Caribbean folk saying, 'each one can teach one'. Consequently, throughout my academic career, I have prioritised the recruitment and development of black students – a demographic underrepresented in theological education and academic teaching. For instance, in my first teaching role in Birmingham (1993-1999), I established an Access Course to Higher Education for black students interested in studying academic theology at the Queen's College. One of the many budding theological students who attended some of these sessions was Anthony Reddie, who became the first black theologian to teach at Oxford University. Later while teaching at Birmingham University, (2000-2008), I was responsible for the recruitment and supervision of twenty black PhDs. In Kent, at Canterbury Christ Church University, between 2013-18, in collaboration with the womanist philosopher, Dr Gabriella Beckles-Raymond, I established the Woolwich Project. The project was a satellite department of theology based in East London specifically to train clergy from the emerging west African churches in London. At the time of writing, in 2021, I am in a working partnership with Dr Dulcie McKenzie and Dr Gifford Rhamie (two of my former PhD students), to support the education and supervision of the largest cohort of black postgraduate theological students in Britain (70 students) at the Queen's Ecumenical Foundation (formerly the Queen's College) in Birmingham. Regarding the second aspect of my praxis theology, the intertextuality of theological and media texts, as I demonstrate in my monograph, *Documentary as Exorcism: Resisting the Bewitchment of Colonial Christianity* (Bloomsbury, 2014), my media texts have supported the confrontation of a range of social issues including western corporate greed in Africa, reparations for the descendants of the victims of the Trans-Atlantic Slave Trade and the combating of right-wing racist campaigning in London. More recently, in 2021, I worked on a BBC *Panorama* documentary on racism in the Church of England ('Is the Church Racist?'). The day after the broadcast, the Church of England made immediate changes to how the Church addressed acts of racial injustice.[16] Film and media is often a more powerful medium for social conscientisation and political action than writing scholarly articles and books for the theological academy.

My theology

This book is a reflection on three theological concepts and their entanglement with media texts. The three theological concepts, God, Jesus, and the Holy Spirit were initially discussed in previous works between 1998-

[16] See, 'Justin Welby tells Church of England to stop using NDAs amid Racism Claims', BBC News Online, 20 April 2021, https://www.bbc.co.uk/news/uk-56817048

2006, and here I adapt, expand, and collate them as a collection. Each chapter follows a loosely conceived contextual theological method:

1. The chapters begin with a question arising out of lived experience.
2. Next, the lived experience is analysed through sociological-cultural lenses before undergoing a theological reflection.
3. Each chapter ends with an example of action, which, within the specificity of my theology is a specific *media* text (documentary film, radio drama and contemporary gospel music) that I made between 2007-2017.

The media texts are a two-fold praxis. First, getting the projects aired. When I started out, there were few spaces for working class men of African Caribbean heritage working in academia to make politically motivated films for black communities on British television. I was not the face of acceptable blackness at that time: a black former athlete or musician. A black liberation theologian making mainstream documentaries was groundbreaking. Second, the films were praxis because of what they achieved. As noted elsewhere, many had a direct impact on policy, politics, and the liberation of black communities.[17]

Why is my theology called 'Duppy Conqueror?' In Jamaican culture, 'duppy conqueror' denotes, amongst many things, the destruction of malevolent spirits (exorcism) or overturning mistruths. Many people outside of Jamaica first heard this phrase in the 1970s as the title of one of the tracks from The Wailers' album, *Burnin'* (1973). From the location of the black theological academy, I re-cast the term to describe a black theological exorcism. As I show in *Documentary as Exorcism: Resisting the Bewitchment of Colonial Christianity* (2014), exorcism in the New Testament has a close association with anti-colonialism and therefore exorcism is intimately related to

---

[17]   See Robert Beckford, *Documentary as Exorcism*, 2014.·

decolonisation and decoloniality. In the case of my theology, it is the untruths of colonial Christianity that are the focus of my attention. To be a duppy conqueror is 'to drive' out untruths told to enslaved and colonial peoples about the meaning of God in the world and their continuity or coloniality in African Caribbean Christianity in the diaspora. Duppy conqueror is a theology for deliverance from colonial Christianity.

1
God of the Rahtid

I BEGIN WITH the doctrine of God.

The doctrine of God in Christian theology considers the attributes of God as presented in the Hebrew and Greek Scriptures. Today most theological students in Britain are introduced to the study of God through a western philosophical gaze on categories of thought, including God as personal, impassible, theodical, transcendent, immanent, omnipotent, creator and omniscient. Few students, from the outset, are introduced to contextuality as a defining feature of God-talk.[18] Therefore, undergraduate students do not have to comprehend how positioning (socio-political and religious cultural factors) inform theological thought. Few theological students in Britain, in my experience, leave university with awareness

---

[18] Bergmann, Sigurd, and Vähäkangas, Mika, *Contextual Theology: Skills and Practices of Liberating Faith* (Abingdon, Oxon; New York, NY: Routledge, 2021).

of how whiteness or coloniality has informed their theological education.[19] In contrast, in African Caribbean Christian tradition, positionality is primary. Missionary Christianity from Europe and later from North America did not introduce ideas about the Christian God in a neutral or unbiased way in the British-run slave labour camps of Caribbean slavery – on the contrary, the entry of the Christian God is coterminous with racial terror.[20] For this reason, African Caribbean Christians have always had a sensitivity to the interconnection of theological ideas and social location. For blacks in the West Indies, the meaning of God was intimately related to anti-slavery (Sam Sharpe), anti-imperialism (Paul Bogle) and anti-racism (Marcus and Amy Garvey).[21] Fast forward to the 1990s, as a black,

[19] Perkinson, James W., *White Theology: Outing Supremacy in Modernity* (New York: Palgrave Macmillan, 2004); Drexler-Dreis, *Decolonial Theology in the North Atlantic World* (Leiden: Brill, 2019).

[20] Erskine, Noel Leo, *Plantation Church: How African-American Religion was Born in Caribbean Slavery* (New York: Oxford University Press, 2014).

[21] Campbell, Horace, *Rasta and Resistance: From Marcus Garvey to Walter Rodney* (London: Hansib Publications, 2007).

British, heterosexual male, standing within the tradition of African Caribbean history, my interest in the doctrine of God was, like my forebears, similarly positional, because it was invested in black struggle.

What does the meaning of God have to contribute to the ubiquity of racial injustice in Britain? This question was at the forefront of my mind in the early noughties. While my white contemporaries in the theological academy debated the substance of the Trinity, the relationship between Christianity and Science, the meaning of the 'Toronto Blessing', and Christ and culture, I foregrounded the catastrophe of the racial violence visited, both psychologically and physically, on black bodies. Why did I ask this question? Because in the context of late modernity, I witnessed numerous colleagues, friends and family members experience trauma, deep depression and even lose their minds because of racism-induced mental illnesses.[22] Arguably, from the

22 See Bhui, Kamaldeep, *Racism and Mental Health: Prejudice and Suffering* (London: Jessica Kingsley, 2002).

mid-1990s, the black community experienced a collective trauma in the wake of the murder of the black teenager Stephen Lawrence not dissimilar in recent years, to the global outpouring of grief and rage in response to the killing of the African-American George Floyd in America in 2020.[23] The question was not just a matter of developing an orthodoxy but was also consideration for orthopraxy – the meaning of God as anti-racist praxis.[24] In other words, God-talk is not just for the sake of intellectual consistency and 'truthfulness' but also to produce practical action against racialized oppression. God and action are a feature of African Caribbean Christianity.

Knowledge of God is discovered through God's action in the life and events of the believer(s) in African Caribbean Christianity.

[23] hooks, bell, *Killing Rage: Ending Racism* (New York: Henry Holt and Company, 1995); Rowe, Sheila Wise, and Rah, Soong-Chan, *Healing Racial Trauma: The Road to Resilience* (Downers Grove, Illinois: IVP, 2020).

[24] Reddie, Anthony, *Black Theology, Slavery, and Contemporary Christianity* (London; New York: Routledge, 2016).

For instance, in black Pentecostal thought God is defined in terms of God's action in the world instead of relying solely on conceptual abstraction.[25] In sum, an experiential theological epistemology underscores Pentecostal ways of knowing,[26] so that 'who feels it, knows it'. Many of the songs black Pentecostals of the first generation of colonial citizens in Britain (which are also a rich source of theological thought) emphasize God's action in the life of the believer and in the world:

> God is a good god yes he (sic) is
> For he picks me up, and turns me around,
> And plants my feet, on solid ground
> God is a good god, yes he is.

Moreover, through personal experience

---

[25] MacRobert, Iain, *The Black Roots and White Racism of Early Pentecostalism in the USA* (Eugene, Or: Wipf and Stock, 2003); Hollenweger, Walter J., *The Pentecostals* (London: SCM Press, 1972).

[26] Abraham, William J., 'Thinking in Tongues Pentecostal Contributions to Christian Philosophy', *Faith and Philosophy* 29 (2), 2012: 247-250.

believers come to view God as a 'deliverer.' For instance, God is expressed as a protector of the vulnerable. As one chorus puts it:

> Jesus be a fence
> All around me every day
> Lord, I want you to help me
> As I travel along life's way,
> Lord, I know you can, Lord, I know you will
> Fight my battles if I keep still
> Be a fence, all around me every day.

Killing Rage

Nuancing my interest in God-talk, more precisely, I wanted to know who God is for those of us who were angry, vexed, and full of rage because of the experience of the slow drip of micro-aggressive discriminations(s) which corrodes wellbeing and bruises the soul. The trauma born of racialized oppression can lead to unmetabolized anger.[27] Black rage was not expressed homogeneously;

[27] Owens, Lama Rod, *Love and Rage: The Path Of Liberation through Anger* (Berkeley, California: North Atlantic Books, 2020).

because black communities are differentiated by class, gender, sexuality, age, and political orientation. Our lived, intersectional, and trans-dimensional existences mean that all our rage does not come from the same place(s).[28] Black people in Britain deploy various tactics or politics of transfiguration[29] to address the rage born of discrimination. The tactics are on a spectrum of thought and action from the 'separatist discourse' of the Nation of Islam to the 'integrationist discourse' of black conservativism. However, most resistance and re-existence politics in the black community find a home in mainstream liberal politics, which seek civil and legal means of redress, as well as creating supportive spaces and places for the humanizing of black bodies.[30] Back in the 1990s, African Caribbean Christianity

[28] Crenshaw, K.W., Mapping the Margins: Intersectionality, Identity Politics, and Violence Against Women of Color. In K. Crenshaw, N. Gotanda, G. Peller, & K. Thomas (Eds.), *Critical race theory: The key writings that formed the movement* (pp. 357-383). (New York, NY: New Press, 1995).

[29] Williams, Paul, Paul Gilroy (London: Routledge, 2013).

[30] Muir, R. David, and Ade Omooba. 2015. Black church political mobilisation – a manifesto for action. (London: National Church Leaders Forum Publications).

and most of the Black Church tradition in Britain did not have the theological resource to redeem black rage in a meaningful way.

Back in the 90s, black rage in the Black Church was suppressed by two powerful discourses. I term these discourses 'respectability' and 'resisting representation'. Respectability was a spiritual sedative for racialized oppression. Our elders taught us to stay calm, remain dignified and cultivate the fruit of the Spirit (Gal. 5:22-23), especially longsuffering. The second discourse, 'resisting representation', describes an embodied opposition to the angry black person trope.[31] The image of the angry black person is steeped in the long history of violent settler colonialism in the Caribbean and Americas, where suppressing black people was built on the myth of an essentialized black rage. The myth of the angry or animalistic black was integral to the colonial regime's brutal 'seasoning' or

---

[31] Metzl, Jonathan, *The Protest Psychosis: How Schizophrenia Became a Black Disease* (Boston, Mass.: Beacon Press, 2010).

'breaking in' of enslaved peoples, especially black women.[32] In the 90s, in African Caribbean churches, a fear of being seen as 'too angry' and de facto 'too black' in the face of discrimination produced a 'protest phobia'. Our response was to live out and enact a black Christian coolness, instead of expressing a verbal or physical anger towards racial attacks.

The suppression of black Christian rage was theologically problematic. Our passivity signified what we believed about God's action in the world. Because we had no comment on racialized attack, we gave the impression that God was either too far removed from our situation (transcendent, Ps 57:5; 97:9) to notice, or just indifferent (impassible). The consequence of both theological signifiers is a catastrophe: they registered that the meaning of God was incompatible with our anger over injustice, and therefore there was no point getting upset about it in the first place.

---

[32] Dadzie, Stella, *Kick in the Belly: Women, Slavery and Resistance*, (Verso, 2021); Petley, Christer, *White Fury: A Jamaican Slaveholder and the Age of Revolution* (2018).

Overturning the suppression of rage was essential to reconstructing the meaning of God so that theology speaks into black rage. The pathway for a new vision was twofold. First, to reconceptualize rage as a redemptive force in Christian experience – what I term *redemptive vengeance*. Second, to correlate redemptive vengeance with a black experience of rage to conceive of a God who is on the side of those with righteous rage or a *God of the Rahtid.*

Redemptive vengeance

In the Bible, rage is a justified response to injustice. In the New Testament, Jesus expresses anger when faced with the predatory merchants in the temple:

> And they came to Jerusalem. And he entered the temple and began to drive out those who sold and those who bought in the temple, and he overturned the tables of the money-changers and the seats of those who sold pigeons.
>
> (Mark 11:15 ESV)

Ultimately, righteous indignation in the face of injustice is not an end. We can get angry, but it should not lead us to sin (Ephesians 4:26). Anger is not to consume us; in fact, it is disturbing to do so (Psalm 37:8). Instead, righteous anger must lead to redemption. The whole of the biblical narrative underscores a redemptive narrative. Salvation history moves from injustice to justice from rage to redemption. For instance, in the Old Testament, God's rage over the downfall of Jerusalem (Psalm 137) is a turning point that signifies a redemptive trajectory, fulfilled in the coming of Christ (Isaiah 49).

Constructive theology and also Rastafarian linguistics helped me to reconstruct God's rage as redemptive vengeance. Constructive theology proposes that theological thought cannot always follow a neat system or remain fixed in time, oblivious to context, power relations or social issues.[33] God-talk, therefore,

[33] Wyman, Jason A., *Constructing Constructive Theology: And Introduction Sketch* (Minneapolis: Fortress Press, 2017).

is developed and redeveloped in concert with human experience and the traditional sources of theological knowledge (Scripture, tradition, etc.). In other words, humans have the creative flexibility to re-imagine God in Scripture and tradition in response to the prevailing issues, concerns and needs. Within this framework, theology is an evolving cartographical project (a guide) rather than a statute or fixed in stone.[34] The Rastafarian linguistic practice contributes another theological consideration: the role of language in diaspora religious communities. In Rastafari, decolonising theology is also the decolonisation of theological language. Rastafari advocates engagement in numerous linguistic strategies to project new meanings onto existing words (dread) or create new linguistic concepts (I and I) to reflect the unchartered waters of black religious experience.[35] Particularly helpful was

[34] Jones, Serene., *Constructive Theology: A Contemporary Approach to Classical Themes* (Minneapolis, Minn.: Fortress Press), 9.

[35] Pollard, Velma., *Dread Talk: The Language of Rastafari* (Montreal and Kingston: McGill-Queen's University Press, 2009).

the Rastafari's production of neologism such as 'livity', 'outer-national' and 'bo bo'. Both the constructive theology's approach to theology and Rastafari's decolonial 'language games,' inspired me to re-envision God's redemptive rage through the new category of 'redemptive vengeance.'

Redemptive vengeance comprises the compounding of two concepts. First, 'redemption.' Redemption in the Christian tradition is God's plan of salvation in and through the atoning work of Christ – in life and death. Yet in black Caribbean Christian experience, especially those still 'bewitched' by missionary Christianity, there is a tendency to reduce redemption to personal salvation and personal piety – although Scripture depicts redemption as holistic and total. Therefore, redemption is better understood as a totality, with something to contribute to all aspects of creation and humanity (Rom. 8:22-24). Next, 'vengeance' here, describes a way of thinking about how God addresses the wrath of God (Rom. 12:19-21). I fold vengeance into

41

God's wrath against injustice (Deut. 32:35). Therefore, 'redemptive vengeance' describes God's rage against injustice as a redemptive, transformative, and empowering force in human history.

The central characteristics of redemptive vengeance are that it is holistic and intersectional. Redemptive vengeance engages in all aspects of black life. Redemptive vengeance does not, for example, neglect the internal problems within the black community. For example, redemptive vengeance is the subplot in my study of lateral violence in black communities (*God and the Gangs*, 2004). An intersectional redemptive vengeance means that redemptive vengeance engages in analyses that intersect categories of discrimination (race, class, gender, sex, etc.). Redemptive vengeance identifies the grim reality that many of the victims within our communities are women and children. Domestic violence, neglect and abuse are unhealthy areas of life that must be addressed. In sum, redemptive vengeance contends equally with external injustice and

42

the internal problems we face. Redemptive vengeance also acknowledges that these two categories (internal/external) are not mutually exclusive, as all black life takes place inside longstanding historical power-relations that have worked to obfuscate (hide) or exacerbate (make worse) pre-existing conditions of neglect and disadvantage.

'Redemptive vengeance' has implications for the meaning of God. Redemptive vengeance has resonance with the understanding of God as immanent and passible. Immanence describes God's presence and rule over history and experience (Gen 21:22; 26:28). In the immanence modality, the being of God is within this world, and language and understanding can contribute something to the understanding of God. Redemptive vengeance affirms a God who is active in human affairs and who desires to intervene – in God's time. Redemptive vengeance is both 'now and not yet.' It is for this time (Romans 1:18-32) and at the end of time (Matthew 24). Redemptive vengeance is also an expression of the passibility of God — the doctrine that describes God as experiencing the feelings of humanity. Redemptive vengeance underlines that 'God cares'. As Jurgen Moltmann put it:

> A God who cannot suffer is poorer than any man [sic]. For a God who is incapable of suffering is a being who cannot be involved. Suffering and injustice do not affect him. And because he is so completely insensitive, he cannot be affected or shaken by anything. He cannot weep, for he has no tears. But the one who cannot suffer cannot love either. So he is a loveless being.[36]

God of the Rahtid

Redemptive vengeance is an aspect of God that makes its point of departure those who rage with righteous anger. Another way of

[36] Moltmann, Jürgen, *The Crucified God: The Cross of Christ as the Foundation and Criticism of Christian Theology*, trans. R. A. Wilson and John Bowden (New York: Harper & Row, 1974), 222.

describing God as a God on the side of those who get vexed about oppression is that God is a 'God of the Rahtid'. God of the Rahtid is the product of a correlation of the Jamaican word 'rahtid' and redemptive vengeance. Rahtid is a term derived from the Jamaican language for 'wrath'. In Jamaican diaspora culture, 'rahtid' is used as an exclamation, 'rahtid!' It can register the experience of shock, anger and even awe. Rahtid's association with anger is of interest here. When Rahtid is correlated with redemptive vengeance, it communicates the vision of a God who understands our rage, participates in it, and sides with us as we engage in redemptive action.

A *God of the Rahtid* is articulated in my visual media projects, including television documentary filmmaking. For example, in 2006, I presented the television documentary *Ghetto Britain* to confront the neo-Nazi British National Party.[37] The film was a critique of

[37] See *Ghetto Britain*, Channel 4 (2006). https://www.channel4.com/programmes/ghetto-britain-30-years-of-race/on-demand/41820-0010

state-sponsored multi-culturalism which produced policies and practices that divided communities rather than building on Britain's convivial culture. The film also examined how state-sponsored multiculturalism failed to engage with white communities and left them vulnerable to the racist policies of right-wing extremist groups, including the British National Party in the London Borough of Dagenham. Confronting the British National Party in Dagenham was the high point of redemptive vengeance in the film. Pandering to the fears of the whites, racist groups sent out flyers and other publications with misinformation about local housing policies, including the outlandish claim that the Local Authority was gifting African families £40k for moving into the area. This misinformation was the source of distress in the local black community and induced fear and anxiety. In the mise-en-scène, redemptive vengeance was trained upon exposing the truth of the situation. In one sequence, I confronted the leader of the British National Party in the area about the misinformation they were spreading and the potentially devastating impact on community relations. A few days afterwards, the Party withdrew the pamphlet, and with the negative publicity that ensued, lost the local election campaign. Rage channelled into anti-racism is the way of a *God of the Rahtid*.

2

Jesus is Dread

THE SECOND SUBJECT is Christology.

Christological study contends with who Jesus was, is, and will be in the future. Each generation must contend with Mark 8:20, 'But who do you say that I am?' To answer this question classic Christological categories of inquiry, include the person of Christ (son of God, Messiah, etc.), the work of Christ (salvation), the meaning of the resurrection and Christ as a model of a godly life. African Caribbean Christianity as a colonial faith inherits many of these classic considerations. Still, as was the case with the doctrine of God, my concern was how to rethink Christology in response to the distinctive historical and cultural history of the Caribbean diaspora in Britain.

Jesus in African Caribbean Diaspora Christianity

To develop a contextual Christology we must reckon with two powerful discourses on the persons and work of Jesus in African Caribbean Christianity. One emerges from the theomusical tradition of African Caribbean diaspora 'back home' choruses, and the other from the revolutionary exploits of enslaved and colonised peoples in Caribbean history. The theology of the songs of the 'back home' choruses that were transported from the Caribbean to Britain signified on longstanding images of Jesus as saviour, surrogate relative and healer.

Jesus as a saviour in African diaspora Christianity, especially in Pentecostal traditions, is more than a concept, or historical event; Jesus as saviour is an experience of faith. In other words, salvation is embodied, expressed as a loving relationship, and often extends into the experience of the second blessing or infilling of the Holy Spirit. As one chorus states:

I love that man, from Galilee
For he has done so very much for me

He has taken away all my sins
And let the Holy Ghost come in
I love that man from Galilee.

The Jesus of the 'back home' choruses also present a surrogate relative image of Christ, where a personal Christ fulfils every familial role in the life of the believer:

He is every, every everything to me
He is every, every everything to me
He is my mother and my father, and my
    sister and my brother
He is everything to me.

For a people who endured a history of forced separation from their homeland and later as enslaved peoples, lived under the daily threat of forced separation of children from parents, and wives from husbands, a universal surrogate kin role for Jesus is a powerful re-reading of the Jesus of history.

Finally, Jesus as a healer is expressed in a chorus that retells the healing ministry of Christ in the gospels:

> Everywhere he went my Lord he was doing
> good
> He is a mighty healer, he cleansed the leper
> When the people saw him, they started
> walking
> Everywhere he went my Lord he was doing
> good.

Another Christology, however, emerges from Christian praxis played out in the brutal underside of Church history. The second Christology is constituted to confront slavery's racial capitalism and racial terror. In this alternate spiritual universe, Jesus is *lived* as emancipator. Jesus is experienced as an emancipator because he came to save (Matthew 16:13-17). Jesus as emancipator describes Jesus as the 'messiah' whose work in the world was freedom. Freedom was not only spiritual but also material – Jesus the Messiah also frees from the sin of the occult slave system.[38] Jesus as messiah is exemplified in Christian-

---

[38] Thomas, Oral A. W., *Biblical Resistance Hermeneutics Within a Caribbean Context,* 2014, pp. 27-46.

led revolutionary praxis in Caribbean history. Revolutionary praxis begins with the enslaved Christian preachers of the nineteenth century, and later it is embodied in the Christian-led anti-colonial resistance across the region. The early slave-led churches of Sam Sharpe and the latter anti-colonial struggle of Paul Bogle are predicated on the far-reaching image of Christ as emancipator. After emancipation from slavery in 1934/8, the vision of Christ the emancipator is reconfigured in the actions of the early twentieth-century Baptist leader, Alexander Bedward, and in the Black Atlantic, the religious musings of the Universal Negro Improvement Association (UNIA). Both Bedward and UNIA folded racial justice themes into Christology. For Bedward, Christ would smash the white wall of oppression, and the UNIA 'Christ for Africans' would come about through an Afri-centric gaze on Scripture.

African Caribbean Christology in Britain carries the weight of Caribbean Christian history. On the one hand, even though second and third-generation African Caribbean

Christians may not sing the 'back home' choruses as frequently as the first generation, the theomusicological images of Jesus persist in the life of the church.[39] That is to say, Jesus remains a saviour, friend, and healer, with no attendant socio-political consideration. On the other hand, the dissenting tradition did not gain a foothold in diaspora churches. Instead, Jesus as emancipator is only envisioned in terms of Christian biopolitics or piety. Emancipation becomes the domain of deliverance from personal 'sin' rather than addressing the 'sins' of the system. Only twentieth-century Rastafari in the Caribbean and Caribbean diaspora retains the revolutionary rhetoric and praxis of an emancipatory black messiah.[40]

Many black Christians of my generation lived the intersection of these two Christologies in our faith experience. Inside the

[39] McLean-Farrell, Janice A. , *West Indian Pentecostals* (London: Bloomsbury Academic, 2017).

[40] Chevannes, Barry, *Rastafari Roots and Ideology* (Syracuse, NY: Syracuse University Press, 2018); Beckford, Robert, *Dread and Pentecostal: A Political Theology for the Black Church in Britain* (London: SPCK, 2000).

church, we experienced the African Caribbean
Jesus in song and sermon. Outside of the
church, as members of the black community we
longed for an emancipatory Jesus to provide us
with the necessary inspiration and resources
to organise and confront structural injustice.
The tension between a passive Christianity
and revolutionary black messiah is visualized
in Sonia Boyce's watercolour, 'Missionary
Positions II' (see p.58). In one of the few
images representing black women's faith
stories, the artist uses herself as the model for
two contrasting images of black religion in the
1980s. The first has her praying as a passive
black Christian, and the other (red) signifies
the aesthetics of Rastafari resistance.

As a second-generation black British
Christian, in the late 1990s, I wanted to revive
and reorient the emancipatory Christology of the
nineteenth and early-twentieth- century African
Caribbean Christians towards the prevailing
cultural milieu of black Britain. As mentioned
in the previous chapter, instead of viewing
African Caribbean Christianity, especially,

black Pentecostalism as being outside of the struggle for racial justice, I wanted to articulate an image of God (righteous rage) that had resonance with the black predicament (rahtid). Applying the same method to Christology, I set about constructing a *dread Christ.*

Correlation/Citing Up

To reconsider the meaning of Jesus in the context of second-generation African Caribbean experience, I was drawn to the theological method of correlation and ontological symbols. Correlation is a dialogic method developed by the theologian Paul Tillich (1886-1965).

> It [correlation] tries to correlate the questions implied in the situation with the answers implied in the message ... It correlates questions and answers, situation and message, human existence, and divine manifestation.[41]

The method comprises of a question-and-answer process between the human predicament and theology. In correlation, however, the Christian tradition is dominant in the conversation, and the response must not contradict it.

Correlation as a method, in its basic sense, is not new to Caribbean people. In many respects, the Rastafarian hermeneutic or 'citing up' has identification with corelation's questioning and answering dynamic. Reggae superstar Bob Marley, for instance, deploys a correlation/'citing up' hermeneutic in his songs to reflect the folding of present concerns into Scripture to provide concrete answers:

[41] Tillich, Paul, *Systematic Theology Volume 1*, (Chicago, Ill.: Univ. of Chicago Press, 2009), p. 8.

By citing-up the historical, social, political, and economic context of slavery, colonialism, racism, and oppression as *seen* through the lens of biblical text, in dialogue with the narrative and images of extra-biblical texts, Marley chants down the evil of Babylon, while casting our gaze to hope in Zion.[42]

Tillich's interpretation of religious symbols was also instructive. Tillich describes religious symbols as having multiple functions.[43] Symbols represent something else, and they participate in the reality to which they point; they create new ways of understanding that were otherwise foreclosed; are never neutral and have transformative power, that is, through participation, they 'open up hidden

---

[42] Christopher J. Duncanson-Hales, 'Dread Hermeneutics: Bob Marley, Paul Ricœur and the Productive Imagination', Black Theology (2017), 15:2, 156-175. p.175.

[43] 'Existential Analysis and Religious Symbols' in Basilus, H. A. (ed.), *Contemporary Problems of Religion* (1956) 37f; cf. Herberg, W., *Four Existential Theologians* (1958), 306f.

depths of our own being'.[44] Yet symbols are not everlasting; they are time-locked and temporary. In other words, symbols are limited.[45] To revive the emancipatory tradition of Jesus, I correlated the emancipatory Jesus or messiah with the concept of 'dread'. A dread Christ of black faith was a symbol to invite believers into a new relationship with the work of Christ in the world that was otherwise foreclosed.

Dread

'Dread' in Rastafari is usually associated with the distinctive dreadlocks, worn as a symbol of adherence to the faith.[46] But the aesthetic has a political and linguistic history. Politically, dreadlocks signified separation from the mainstream Babylon system and its Eurocentric expectations for the grooming of black hair. While the historical origins

[44] Tillich, P., *Systematic Theology,* vol. 2 (London, 1953), p. 131.

[45] Tillich, P., *Theology of Culture* (New York, 1964) p. 56.

[46] Edmonds, Ennis Barrington, *Rastafari: A Very Short Introduction* (Oxford: Oxford University Press, 2012), p. 42.

of dreadlocks are disputed,[47] the notion of 'dreadness' in Rastafari has come to symbolise a way of describing the natural Rastafarian 'livity' or way of life.[48] Dread also denotes a range of linguistic functions incorporating both positive and negative meanings. On the one hand, dread is the experience of coming to religious and cultural consciousness. On the other, it can denote divine judgment on oppressors. [49] When I first considered the correlation, the term 'dread' had undergone an evolution of meaning in black British culture. 'Dread' also had the connotation of black consciousness and action. To be dread was to be awakened to the social and political realities confronting black people

[47] Barnett, Michael, *The Rastafari Movement: A North American and Caribbean Perspective* (2018), pp. 84-5.

[48] Edmonds, Ennis B., *Rastafari: A Very Short Introduction*, p. 47ff.

[49] Hepner, Randall L., 'Chanting Down Babylon in the Belly of the Beast: The Rastafarian Movement in the Metropolitan United States', in Murrell, Nathaniel Samuel; Spencer, William David, and McFarlane, Adrian Anthony, *Chanting Down Babylon: The Rastafari Reader* (Philadelphia, Pa: Temple University Press, 1998), p. 211.

and committed to doing something about it.[50]

What new understanding of Jesus emerges when we correlate dread with the reading strategy and experience in Caribbean history that produces the emancipatory Jesus? The answer is a Christ who participates in black struggle in Britain. I suggest three symbols which contour the way of the dread Christ.

Decoloniality, Uplift and Empowerment

A dread Christ is a symbol of decoloniality. As I show elsewhere, Jesus' work of exorcism in the New Testament has anti-colonial sentiment.[51] Driving out demons in New Testament Scholarship registers the removal of the invading Roman colonial forces present in the body of Israel. Jesus' anti-colonial exorcism, therefore, has identification with decoloniality - the drilling out of the oppressive colonial residue in black life. For instance, in

---

[50] Pollard, Velma, *Dread Talk: The Language of Rastafari*, 2nd edn. (Montreal and Kingston: McGill-Queen's University Press, 2000), p.xiii

[51] Beckford, Robert, *Documentary As Exorcism.*

Caribbean educational history, decoloniality seeks to drive out the oppressive 'ways of knowing' that do damage to black minds and bodies in the contemporary world – the epistemic violence of the coloniality of the educational system. Therefore, to say Jesus is dread in theological education in Britain today is to say that Jesus wants, and we struggle for, a more inclusive and liberative theological canon. In regards to theological education, a dread Christ is decolonial – casting out the knowledge of violence against black people.

A dread Christ is a symbol of a Christ of black upliftment. Jesus as an uplifter is evident in his mission for equality and justice amongst the least of these (Matthew 24), especially marginalised women (John 4:1-42) and outcasts (Luke 14:15-24). African Caribbean people have a strong tradition of viewing Jesus' message of salvation as upliftment, individually, but less of a track record of contending with uplift for black people(s). A dread Christ, therefore, as uplifter, cannot disengage from the issues that have oppressed

black people. The followers of a dread Christ
must engage with black history, cultures, and
contest with every force of non-being that
comes up against black people. A dread Christ
is not silent on reparations, neo-colonialism in
the Caribbean or Africa, and the struggle for
justice for the Windrush generation. Neither
is a dread Christ immune to the ubiquitous
anti-blackness in the global media dressed up
as 'culture wars'. However, black uplift does
not come at the expense of other bodies – the
way of the dread Christ is not a reversal of the
racialised binary opposition of black and white
bodies in the history of western Christianity.
Neither is the dread of Christ homophobic.
Instead, the way of the Christ of black uplift
is womanist, in the sense that a dread Christ
seeks to empower all of creation and all the
human family.[52]

A dread Christ is also a Christ of black empowerment. Empowerment is praxis. Tradition-
ally, empowerment in African Caribbean Chris-

[52]   Coleman, Monica A., *Making a Way Out of No Way: A
Womanist Theology* (Minneapolis: Fortress Press), 2008.

tianity has focused on deliverance and healing as spiritual empowerment. For a dread Christ, however, the healing power of God is extended into social concerns. In this regard, healing for the dread Christ has identification with black liberation as a socio-political praxis.

Media: Dramatizing the Dread Christ

A dread Christ is represented in the 2017 radio drama, *Jesus Piece*. *Jesus Piece* is a fictitious story of a revolutionary black pastor living and working in the inner city of Birmingham who seeks to live out the dread Christ's vision of decoloniality, uplift and empowerment. I originally conceived the idea in 2012, and with the support of the dramatist, actor, and theatre impresario, Kwame Kwei-Armah, produced a one-hour BBC3 radio drama in 2013. The television film star, David Harewood fronted our programme, which was broadcast as *Father, Son and Holy Ghost* (2013).[53] However, I further developed the idea for BBC Radio Regions

[53] *Father, Son and Holy Ghost*, BBC Radio 2 (2013). https://www.bbc.co.uk/programmes/b01d0vb0

in 2016 with the writing support of the African British writer Sarah Chukwudebe. The four-part series, *Jesus Piece*, was broadcast on the BBC Radio regions in 2017.

Jesus Piece tells the story of Pastor Toussaint, a black pastor in Birmingham who after a rocky start in life, converts to Christianity and is called to the ministry. His version of Christianity is shaped and informed by the revolutionary black Christianity of the nineteenth-century Caribbean dissenting tradition. The jazz musician Soweto Kinch (see photo on p.68) stars as Pastor Toussaint, and the narrative is built around a murder in the black community:

The gripping story is set in Birmingham and centres around Toussaint – a reformed gang member who finds God and becomes a Pastor ... After being appointed Pastor in a broken community Toussaint – known as Pastor T – quickly builds bridges and makes a difference, especially amongst young, black worshippers. But because of his past, the established church elders don't approve. When he is accused of murder a gripping tale unfolds leaving

listeners hooked right the way through to the last instalment.

Folding the dread Christ into *Jesus Piece* makes contemporaneous the dread Christ and criminology. Within this re-telling of Christology, the locus of the dread Christ is the criminalisation of black youth, police indifference to black suffering and the role of the Black Church as an agent of radical change. Furthermore, Pastor Toussaint embodies a vision of Christianity that is as equally at home saving souls for Christ through evangelism as it is with confronting racist police and corrupt local authority officials. In short, the narrative of *Jesus Piece* presents a symbol of a dread Christ, which invites all committed to justice and equality by participating in a dread salvific trajectory to make right the historical injustices visited on large sections of black people.

3
Spirit Dub

THE FINAL SUBJECT is the Holy Spirit.

I was raised in a Christian culture dominated by an acute spiritual consciousness. At church, we sang a multitude of songs about the Holy Spirit. At home, our parents told us Jamaican 'duppy' stories and other tales of supernatural spirits roaming the universe.[54] I will never forget one set of duppy stories, concerning a deceased relative, because they were so terrifying even for a 'mannish' inner-city young teen. Though, every duppy story ended with a promise of protection for living relatives. These stories served a dual role of cultural retention and political commentary. For colonial citizens like my parents and some of my sisters born

---

[54] Hausman, Gerald, *Duppy Talk: West Indian Tales of Mystery And Magic* (Pine Island, Fla: Irie Books, 2006); Araya, Karla, 'Anancy stories beyond the moralistic approach of the western philosophy of being', BLO 4 (2014), pp.43-52.

in Jamaica, duppy stories signified an African heritage (storytelling and cosmology), and like Anancy stories, they were, on a subliminal level, social commentaries on colonial and postcolonial power relationships.[55]

Our family never considered the intersections of these two traditions of the supernatural: the overlapping categories of experiencing the Jamaican spiritual world and the Holy Spirit's role in confronting evil, especially structural evil. With this distinctive spirituality in the rear-view of African Caribbean Christianity, it is no wonder that sensitivity to the work of the Spirit is a theological distinctive of Pentecostal churches.[56]

Pneumatology was strategic for reorienting the theology of African Caribbean Christianity towards the transformation of the social world. Pneumatology is the study of the Holy Spirit in

[55] Onuora, Adwoa Ntozake, *Anansesem: Telling Stories and Storytelling African Maternal Pedagogies* (Bradford, ON: Demeter Press, 2015).

[56] Sturge, Mark, *Look What the Lord has Done!: An Exploration of Black Christian Faith in Britain* (Bletchley: Scripture Union, 2005).

Scripture and history. While much of western scholarship has focused on the Spirit's role in the Godhead, in African Caribbean Christianity, especially black Pentecostalism, pneumatology is an experience – the dynamics of the infilling of the Holy Spirit.

My interest in pneumatology in the early 2000s was socio-political. I wanted to conceive of the work of the Spirit in the world in relation to structural change. To envision the Spirit as socially engaged contradicts the experience of the Spirit in African Caribbean Christianity, where the locus of the work of the Spirit is the body. Hence the emphasis in African Caribbean Pentecostal churches on the experience of the infilling of the Spirit.[57]

Dub Method

Reggae musicology provided me with a cultural approach to rework pneumatology, specifically 'dub'. 'Dub' is a reggae music

[57] Hollenweger, Walter J., and MacRobert, Iain, *The Black Roots and White Racism of Early Pentecostalism in the USA* (Palgrave Macmillan, 2014).

mixing technique where the original track of a record is deconstructed and reconstructed under the creative genius of a music producer. Taking the lead from dub method, we can re-conceive the theological task as 'dub,' that is, a two-fold process.

1. Deconstruction or re-evaluation of the central components of pneumatology, in the African Caribbean Pentecostal tradition.
2. Reconfiguring of the components inspired by the signature style of the 'producer/ theologian' to present a new understanding of the work of the Spirit.

As John S. McClure, shows in *Mashup Religion: Pop Music and Theological Invention*, technologized music production techniques are a rich source of material for theological invention.[58] In this case, the signature style is

---

[58] McClure, John S., *Mashup Religion: Pop Music and Theological Invention* (Waco, Texas: Baylor University Press, 2011).

informed by an understanding of the Spirit at the Azusa Street Revival of 1906.

Deconstruction

Scripture leaves us with no concise treatment of the work of the Spirit, which, as constructive theologians remind us, is not an irregular situation for most of the dominant themes in Scripture.[59] What we do have in Scripture are images and concepts of the Spirit which gesture towards an experiential pneumatology rather than a strict doctrinal formulation. The six primary images of the Spirit in the Bible are life-breath, wind, fire, water, dove and the paraclete. African Caribbean Christianity, especially black Pentecostals, are not solely invested in philosophical speculation over the third person of the Trinity but also with the experience of the Spirit in the body and as spiritual gifts – what the Spirit does

---

[59] Wyman, Jason A., *Constructing Constructive Theology: An Introductory Sketch* (2017); Jones, Serene, *Constructive Theology: A Contemporary Approach to Classical Themes* (Minneapolis, Minn: Fortress Press, 2008).

in the world today.[60] Consequently, black Pentecostals take as a canon within the canon Acts: 2:1-4):

> When the day of Pentecost came, they were all together in one place. Suddenly a sound like the blowing of a violent wind came from heaven and filled the whole house where they were sitting. They saw what seemed to be tongues of fire that separated and came to rest on each of them. All of them were filled with the Holy Spirit and began to speak in other tongues as the Spirit enabled them. (NIV)

Derived from Acts is a twofold emphasis on the work of the Spirit as personal empowerment and supernatural gifting. The presence of the Holy Spirit as personal empowerment is reflected in song. Take, for instance the image of the Spirit as empower in the chorus, 'Fire, Fire, Fire':

---

[60] Wariboko, Nimi, and Yong, Amos, *Paul Tillich and Pentecostal Theology Spiritual Presence and Spiritual Power* (Bloomington, Ind: Indiana University Press, 2015).

Fire, fire fire, fire fall on me
On the day of Pentecost
Fire fall on me
On the day of Pentecost
Fire fall on me.

The Holy Spirit is also experienced as in supernatural gifts such as the production of divine knowledge (1 Cor. 2:10). Divine knowledge or supernatural revelation is communicated to individuals through an encounter with the Holy Spirit such as receiving a prophetic word or the interpretation of an unknown tongue. Divine communication represents a counter-hegemonic epistemology or way of knowing which privileges non-rationalist modalities.[61]

African Caribbean pneumatology reflects both the strengths and weaknesses of black spirituality. Its strength is the capacity of the Spirit to transform the individual's way of thinking and being in the world. Transformation, however, is contained: its focus is personal and individual

---

[61] Smith, James K. A.. *Thinking in Tongues: Pentecostal Contributions to Christian Philosophy* (2010).

empowerment, and no more. As Valentina Alexander's analysis of the predicament puts it, African Caribbean spirituality is a lived tension or 'passive-radicalism'. Passive radicalism describes an implicit application of the Spirit's power, which inadvertently evades socio-political consideration:

Liberational spirituality is, therefore, the key epistemological tool ... it has most often been, however, essentially an *implicit* tool enabling believers to identify, challenge and overcome the various levels of their ideological and material oppression *without necessarily seeking out its socio-historical source and without making an explicit theological alignment with that liberational process.* To the extent that this manifestation of social analysis ... it has been identified in this study as *passive radicalism.* [62] [italics mine]

---

[62] Alexander, V. *'Breaking Every Fetter'? To What Extent Has the Black Led Church in Britain Developed a Theology Of Liberation?* (Ph.D thesis, University of Warwick, 1997), p.227.

Alexander offers 'active radicalism' as an alternative to passive radicalism. Active-radicalism projects the transforming power of African Caribbean spirituality into the social world to confront structural and material causes of black distress. Active radicalism applied to pneumatology in African Caribbean congregations imbues pneumatology with a social value. Take, for instance the power of the Spirit in the healing rites of African Caribbean congregations. The desire to pray, anoint or the laying on of hands for spiritual healing for bodily disease could equally apply to a refocusing of the Spirit's power on the 'social body' so that the power of the Holy Ghost confronts social diseases such as racism, poverty, homophobia or sexism.

Reconstruction

To remix or 'dub' pneumatology, I appropriate as my signature style an alternative image of the Spirit from the history of Pentecostalism. A socio-political reading of the Azusa Street Revival offers an alternative evaluation of the meaning and work of the Spirit. A socio-political interpretation is a gaze on history cognisant of the attitudes and ideas that change the way people act and live and how these changes negotiate power relationships in the social world. Within the specificity of the study of the Holy Spirit, we ask ourselves the question, 'After the experience of the Holy Spirit what social and political transformation took place as a consequence at the Azusa Street Revival?'

The Azusa Street Revival of 1906 is credited as the birth of classic western Pentecostalism.[63] The chief architect was the African-American preacher William J. Seymour. Seymour was a descendant of enslaved Africans, who became a student of the white Pentecostal preacher, Charles Fox Parham. From Parham, Seymour learned of the baptism of the Spirit as evidence of a third work of grace (preceding salvation and sanctification). Seymour sought

[63] Anderson, Allan, *An Introduction to Pentecostalism: Global Charismatic Christianity* (Cambridge: Cambridge University Press, 2016).

to realise this doctrine, and after weeks of preaching and prayer at North Bonnie Brae Street, their faith was rewarded with the Spirit's baptism. News spread quickly of this phenomenon, and to accommodate the upsurge in interest in receiving the baptism of the Holy Spirit the Azusa Street Mission was established in the industrial quarter of Los Angeles. Over the next six years, thousands of people experienced the baptism of the Holy Spirit, and other miraculous happenings such as supernatural healings.

A socio-political reading of the Azusa Revival foregrounds the social and political transformations concurrent with the arrival of the Spirit. Running parallel with this new pneumatology is an anti-oppressive Christian praxis. First, inter-racial fellowship is affirmed and practised as a sign of the presence of the Holy Spirit – in radical contrast to the highly segregated societies across the West Coast of America at the turn of the century. There was also an anti-sexist practice. Women played a prominent role in the ministry and were appointed leaders. For instance, after Seymour's death, his wife was appointed 'Bishop' over the fellowship. An anti-classism accompanied the anti-sexist praxis. A profound sense of social equality is registered in the seating arrangements:

> Worshippers gathered in a new way completely equal in the house of God, the body of Christ not a collection of individuals looking over the back of many heads simply to the clergy or choir but an intimate whole serving one another. This unconventional seating plan revealed Seymour's conviction that events transpiring at Azusa Mission were different, unique and revolutionary.[64]

Therefore, Azusa gives expression to the presence and work of the Spirit as a liberating force that confronts and overturns social inequalities.

---

[64] Nelson, D. J., *For Such a Time as This: The Story of Bishop William J. Seymour and the Azusa Street Revival* (Unpublished Ph.D. dissertation, University of Birmingham, May 1981), p. 120.

Does biblical pneumatology reflect the work of the Spirit as socio-political? Hispanic theologian Eldin Villafane confirms the social dimensions of the work of the Spirit in his reflection on the image of the Spirit in the New Testament as personal/vertical and social/horizontal. As Villafane puts it, the Spirit's work is twofold:

> ... personal transformation/piety (prayer mystic, contemplation, thus inner-directed and vertical). And the horizontal: social transformation/piety (justice, advocacy, social action, thus outer-directed and horizontal).[65]

Villafane offers two images of the Spirit from the New Testament to illustrate the horizontal trajectory. These are *grieving* and *brooding*. The first category is useful because it describes the theological basis for a socio-political pneumatology. The Spirit's grieving (Ephesians

[65]   Ibid., p.165.

4:30 and 5:1-2) is a way of describing how 'sin', especially the failure to practise Christian love, grieves the Spirit. For Villafane, the grieving of the Spirit is caused by sin that is both personal and social. While the personal originates in the fall of humanity (Genesis 1-3) and results in separation from God (Romans 6:23a),[66] social sin is seen in the unjust organisation of human society. When wrongly and unjustly organised, social organizations and practices provide evil with an opportunity to manifest itself in social structures such as education, employment, and policing.

Villafane's argument suggests that to follow Jesus and reject sin is also an implicit rejection of sin's social manifestations whether in racism, sexism, classism or unjust laws. [67] Whereas grieving the Spirit enables

[66] Villafane uses the theological concept of *sarx* (flesh) to articulate the theological nature of personal sin. What is important is that sin is also social in that individuals constitute society and a social order produces human beings, in short, social institutions whether family, school, work or state, exhibit a morality.

[67] Villafane, *The Liberating Spirit*, p.191.

the believer to identify sin as a reality in the social world, the Spirit's brooding, the second category, describes how the Spirit is a force for social justice. The Spirit also works in the capacity of restrainer (*to Katechon* – 2 Thess. 2:6, 7) and helper (*parakletos* – John 14:16). The former refers to the defensive work of the Spirit, the way that the Spirit maintains order and restrains the evil powers of this world. The latter refers to the Spirit's offensive role, assisting, teaching and nurturing to usher in the signs of God's reign of love, peace, and justice.[68] Therefore the church as a community filled with the Spirit must involve itself in the defensive and offensive work of the Spirit.[69]

Spirit Dub

Spirit dub is the reconstruction of pneumatology informed by the events at the Azusa Mission. Spirit dub means the work of the Spirit is not confined to the body, but also to the social world – all of God's creation. These

[68] Ibid., p.183.
[69] Ibid., p.187.

new parameters of the work of the Spirit require a new index for measuring the presence of the Spirit. First, in terms of words of knowledge we must question prophetic utterances of the Spirit that refuse to speak truth to power. Second, a church community committed to this holistic pneumatology should be more socially active, more willing to speak against injustice and exhibit a radical corporate inclusion and fellowship of all peoples, no matter what shapes, sizes or genders or sexualities.

Media: Work of the Spirit (Jamaican Bible Remix 2017)

Expression of a holistic pneumatology, that is a practice of the Spirit incorporating the Spirit's work in the whole of the world and

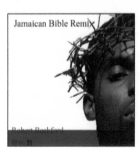

creation is the focus of the song, 'Work of the Spirit' from the *Jamaican Bible Remix* album. The album samples passages from the 'Di Jamiekan

Nyuu Testiment' version of the New Testament (2012), and constructs songs that re-relate the Scripture to contemporary social themes. It is a co(con)textualized, inter-textual interpretation.[70]

The track 'Work of the Spirit' rehearses Villafane's pneumatology. The lyrics of the song tell of the defensive and offensive work of the Spirit. In the visual narrative of the music video, a fictional account is presented of a black female pastor who, inspired by the Spirit, confronts human trafficking in her community. The audio and video content combined, denotes that the work of the Spirit in the world is to defend the weak and attack the oppressor – whoever they are and wherever they are found.

WORK OF THE SPIRIT[71]

ABIGAIL KELLY – What is the work, what's the work of the Spirit?

[70] Smith, Mitzi J. Smith, *Womanist Sass and Talk Back* (Cascade Books, 2018).
[71] See, 'Work of the Spirit', *Jamaican Bible Remix* (2017) https://www.youtube.com/watch?v=mSS7mQ4PPAo

JNT – II Tesaluoniyan 2

Nou, unu don nuo aredi di wan we a uol im bak, an im a-go gwaan uol im bak so im kyan kom wen a fi im taim fi kom. Kaaz wan wikid sitn de bout we a wok anda di kwaiyat fi kaaz piipl fi go gens Gad Laa. Bot sumadi a uol it bak. An di wan we a uol it bak a-go gwaan uol it til im get muuv outa di wie.

Robert – In church people sing many songs about the Holy Spirit. None more evocative than, '*Anointing Fall On Me*'. In this song, the Holy Spirit is presented as a personal empowerment for people. Something they can call upon to strengthen them. It is very personal and very individual. But this isn't the only image of the Spirit. II Thessalonians paints a picture of the Spirit as a defensive force, restraining the evil within the world, and keeping it in check

Chorus
What's the work of the Spirit?
Bot sumadi a uol it bak (x4)

R<small>OBERT</small> – The work of the Spirit isn't just about
individual empowerment
It's also about holding back the terror within
this world
The Spirit is a dam against a tide of wickedness.

Chorus
What's the work of the Spirit?
Bot sumadi a uol it bak (x4)

R<small>OBERT</small> – But the Spirit's work isn't just about
defence; it's also about attack
We need to take this in a different direction.

JNT – Jan 14
An mi a-go aks mi Faada fi sen wan neda
sumadi fi elp unu an de wid unu aal di taim.
fi elp unu
fi elp unu
fi elp unu

R<small>OBERT</small> – Before Jesus goes back to heaven, he
says to the disciples, he is not going to leave
them alone

He will send the comforter; the comforter is
going to be there to help them
And be there to drive them forward

Chorus
Work of the Spirit (x5)

ROBERT –The work of the Spirit is an offensive
force in this world, puts people who believe in
God on the attack
To 'mash up' the forces of wickedness in this
world

Chorus
Work of the Spirit (x4)
So what's the work of the Spirit within this
world? Within this world (x2)
Defense and attack x12

Conclusion
'Outernational'

MY THEOLOGY CANNOT be separated from my Jamaican heritage and forebears, especially my grandparents. But my theology goes beyond them. Despite my grandparents passing before I had the chance to contemplate travelling to visit them in Jamaica, my parents shared essential memories of their parents. The memories identified contradictions in the colonial Christian life – a tension between social reality and spiritual aspiration.

My mother told me how as a child walking with her mother to town in the 1940s and 1950s, she had to stop and curtsey every time they met a white family on the road. The gesture was a mark of respect for their colonial masters. The act of submission was difficult for my grandmother. This was because

Grandmother Maud was a descendant of a Maroon community on the east of the Island. The Maroons fought for freedom from the British in the eighteenth century and Maud 'felt bad' about not having the resource or power to resist.

My father's recollections were full of tales of hardship and impoverishment. His father worked daily for 'pennies' as an agricultural worker, and his mother struggled to raise a houseful of hungry children on a pittance. His father, however, was cognisant of the exploits of the Jamaican Pan-African black nationalist Marcus Garvey. My father recalls how his father hoped that one day Garvey's vision of black emancipation would bear fruit in future generations.

My theology speaks to the longings of my Jamaican grandparents. Unlike me, they had no opportunity to articulate a redemptive vengeance. Neither were they able to think of Christ as a political force for black emancipation. Duppy Conquering theology, placed within this history is therefore, also, 'diasporan' and outernational. It is both a break and continuity with the colonial past. My theology is a conscious decision to continue to struggle with the residue of Empire, but within the postcolonial metropole. But diaspora is not the last word. Through media praxis,[72] I have taken my theology 'outernational' – beyond the boundaries of the British black community. In solidarity with peoples in Ghana, Nigeria, South Africa, Ethiopia, Palestine and Dalit India I have demonstrated the outernational value of the God of the rahtid, the dread Christ and Spirit dub.

[72] See Beckford, Robert, *Documentary as Exorcism* (2014).

Acknowledgements

THANKS ARE DUE to the following for permission to reproduce copyright material:

Tate Images for Missionary Position II by Sonia Boyce (p. 58)

BBC for image of Soweto Kinch from Jesus Piece, photograph by Richard Stonehouse (p. 68)